THE
BREXIT
SOUVENIR
TREASURY

THE BREXIT SOUVENIR TREASURY

FOND MEMORIES OF THE EUROPEAN UNION FOR ANY NOSTALGIC REMAINER

BY

ADAM G GOODWIN
DICKEN GOODWIN
JONATHAN PARKYN

PORTICO

This is an independent publication. It is completely unofficial and unauthorised and, as such, has no connection with the people or persons featured, or with any organisation or individual connected in any way whatsoever with the people or persons featured.

First published in the United Kingdom in 2018 by

Portico
43 Great Ormond Street
London
WC1N 3HZ

An imprint of Pavilion Books Company Ltd
Copyright © Pavilion Books Company Ltd 2018
Text copyright © Yes/No Publishing Services 2018

ISBN 978-1-91162-210-9

A CIP catalogue record for this book is available from the British Library.

10 9 8 7 6 5 4 3 2 1

Reproduction by Rival Colour Ltd, UK
Printed and bound by G. Canale & C. S.p.A., Italy

This book can be ordered direct from the publisher at
www.pavilionbooks.com

THIS BOOK BELONGS TO

···

(NOT THE EUROPEAN UNION ANY MORE)

FOOD

baguette
A type of crusty French white bread, like a loaf of Mothers Pride stretched into the shape of a rounders bat

biscotti
Biscuits

chorizo
A delicious Spanish version of a Cumberland sausage, but orange and all dried up

croissant
Imagine half a Yorkshire Pudding. Eaten with jam or chocolate jam (see *Nutella*)

meatballs
Beefburger balls eaten all over Europe; in Italy they come with long, straight spaghetti hoops. In Sweden they come with furniture

mozzarella
A crazy Italian cheese, like a cross between Dairylea Triangles and Play-Doh

baguette

biscotti

chorizo

croissant

meatballs

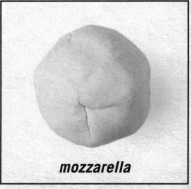
mozzarella

moussaka
Like a Greek shepherd's pie but with aubergines and custard instead of mashed potato

Nutella
Chocolate jam – containing nuts, chocolate and jam

olive oil
Cod liver oil but made with small gooseberry-shaped Mediterranean fruits instead of cod's livers

risotto
A type of rice pudding but with chicken or fish in it and not for pudding

sauerkraut
Like pickled onions, but with cabbage instead of onions

tapas
An indoor picnic

moussaka

nutella

olive oil

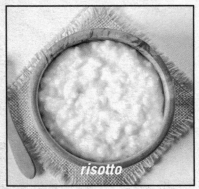
risotto

sauerkraut

tapas

BREXIT SMOOTH FINE QUALITY CIGARETTES

BORIS JOHNSON

No. 1 in a series of 12
MAVERICKS OF BREXIT

BORIS JOHNSON
"BOMBER BORIS"

☒ LEAVER
○ REMAINER

THIS HEAVYWEIGHT DEFENDER OF BRITISH VALUES MAY WELL OFTEN ACT LIKE A BUFFOON BUT HE MANAGED TO SLUG HIS WAY THROUGH THE BREXIT CAMPAIGN AND REMAIN THE LAST MAN STANDING AFTER AN EPIC TWELVE ROUNDS.

HE LASTS LIKE THE COOL FLAVOUR OF A BREXIT SMOOTH.

COLLECTABLE CIGARETTE CARDS

Can you spot a Europhile?

Watch out for the signs:

shares with neighbours
likes single markets
votes 'remain'
believes in free movement

Suspicious?

Call the National Europhilia Watch hotline on 020 0104 2019

UKEA

ENJOY YOUR HOME...

UKEA

After putting up with years of cheap, flat-packed European furniture, we here at UKEA believe in returning to a more traditional, British way of styling your home. Out are the flimsy GNEDBY and the low-cost LIATORP (whatever they are), and in are the sturdy, traditional, dependable, old-fashioned British furniture items we know you'll love.

Your home, the UKEA way...

The Ambassador
A traditional British War Cabinet-style desk

✔ **Mahogany**   ✔ **Brass handles**   ✔ **Nine drawers**
✔ **Lockable top drawer for 'sensitive material'**
✔ **Blue passport compartment**

£2303.00 (p&p £300)

Size: 6ft x 3ft x 3ft-2inches / Weight: 22st 10lb
Please allow 15 weeks delivery as this item comes pre-built

The Imperial
Austere Victorian haunted-house-style bookcase

✔ **Mahogany** ✔ **Twenty-three 'Folio edition-sized' shelves** ✔ **Secret panel for easy escape into room next door**

£8049.00 (p&p £300)

Size: 8ft 3inches x 15ft x 1ft 7inches / Weight: 1 ⅓ tons
Please allow 6 months delivery as this item comes pre-built

The Puritan
Solid wooden Church of England-endorsed bed

✔ **Mahogany** ✔ **British crafted**
✔ **Optional creak for nookie prevention**

£5245.00 (p&p £300)

Size: 8ft x 6ft x 3ft 5inches / Weight: 1 ton
Please allow 9 months delivery as this item comes pre-built
(Blankets and eiderdown not included)

The Beefeater
A heavy upholstered gentleman's chair

✔ **Mahogany** ✔ **British cow-hide leather with brass studs** ✔ **Ideal for entertaining visiting statesmen**

£859.00 (p&p £90)

Size: 3ft 7inches x 1ft 5inches x1ft 5inches / Weight: 2st 3lb
Please allow 12 weeks delivery as this item comes pre-built

The St George
Sturdy and practical Victorian six-member family dinner table

✔ **Mahogany** ✔ **Room for crockery**
✔ **Large area for condiment coverage**
✔ **Flat, even surface**

£6829.00 (p&p £200)

Size: 12ft x 5ft x 4ft / Weight: 42st
Please allow 6 months delivery as this item comes pre-built

Department of Ongoing Euroscepticism

REDACTED INTELLIGENCE REPORT   **CLASSIFIED**

MISSION: TO INVESTIGATE POTENTIAL THREAT TO UK CULTURE
AND WAY OF LIFE POST-BREXIT.

SUBJECT: SWEDEN

FIELD AGENTS: PENNYWEATHER, J
               WHITE, D

REPORT AS FOLLOWS:

Sweden ▬▬▬▬▬▬▬▬▬▬▬▬▬ does not ▬▬▬▬▬
▬▬▬▬▬▬▬▬▬▬ have ▬▬▬▬▬▬▬▬▬
▬▬▬▬▬▬▬▬▬▬▬▬▬▬▬▬▬▬▬
▬▬▬▬▬▬▬▬ an excellent benefits system,
brilliant pop music ▬▬▬▬▬▬▬▬ or ▬▬
▬▬▬▬▬▬▬ stylish ▬▬▬▬▬▬▬▬
flat-packed furniture. ▬▬▬▬▬▬▬▬▬▬
▬▬▬▬▬▬ So ▬▬▬▬▬▬▬▬ there.

TOP SECRET

BREXIT SMOOTH FINE QUALITY CIGARETTES

THERESA MAY

No. 2 in a series of 12
MAVERICKS OF BREXIT

THERESA MAY
"THE SUB"

☒ LEAVER
☒ REMAINER

THIS PERENNIAL SUBSTITUTE HAS SOMEHOW MADE IT TO CAPTAIN OF THE NATIONAL TEAM THOUGH NOBODY SEEMS TO KNOW HOW. AT HOME MOSTLY ON THE RIGHT OF THE PITCH SHE IS KNOWN TO DRIFT INTO ANY POSITION THAT SUITS HER. IN FACT THE ONLY CONSTANT WITH THIS GAL IS HER LOVE OF A COOL BREXIT SMOOTH POST-MATCH.

COLLECTABLE CIGARETTE CARDS

Tackling the five stages of Brexit Grief

1. DENIAL

Symptoms:

- ✔ Headache
- ✔ Insomnia
- ✔ Fluctuating sterling
- ✔ Nausea
- ✔ Numbness
- ✔ Industrial uncertainty
- ✔ Inability to believe you are British

Overview

Denial comes first in the five stages of grief. In this stage, Europe becomes meaningless and overwhelming. We pretend, instead, that we are still part of the EU; that there was no referendum and that things will carry on as normal. This is a way of dealing with the grief. But as the shock subsides we begin to ask ourselves questions. What have we done? What was Cameron doing? Why is Nigel Farage still a thing? This is normal. As the feelings of denial start to fade all the feelings you were denying begin to surface.

Treatment

Prepare a mantra that trains you to face the facts. Something like: We have left – Brexit happened. Now repeat this mantra for all time.

Cure

None.

 **Remainers Health Service**

PRESENTS ...

20 CLASSIC
BREAK-UP 'BREX-HITS'

WALLOW IN THE EXQUISITE PAIN OF GOODBYE
AND SOOTHE AWAY THOSE BREXIT BLUES WITH THIS
ULTIMATE COLLECTION OF TWENTY TEAR-JERKING TRACKS

Without You
HARRY NILSSON

The Way We Were
BARBRA STREISAND

Don't Give Up On Us
DAVID SOUL

All By Myself
ERIC CARMEN

**Hey, That's No Way
To Say Goodbye**
LEONARD COHEN

Bye Bye Love
THE EVERLY BROTHERS

It's Too Late
CAROLE KING

**You've Lost That
Lovin' Feeling**
THE RIGHTEOUS BROTHERS

**I Won't Last A Day
Without You**
THE CARPENTERS

Go Your Own Way
FLEETWOOD MAC

If You Leave Me Now
CHICAGO

**All That's Left Is
To Say Goodbye**
ASTRUD GILBERTO

I Want You Back
JACKSON 5

I Will Survive
GLORIA GAYNOR

Crying
ROY ORBISON

**Sorry Seems To Be
The Hardest Word**
ELTON JOHN

**Fifty Ways To
Leave Your Lover**
PAUL SIMON

Hello Goodbye
THE BEATLES

After The Love Has Gone
EARTH, WIND AND FIRE

Leaving On A Jet Plane
JOHN DENVER

Post-Brexit
Community Notices

FOR SALE

Newly Vacated car plant · includes operational machinery and 3,463 trained staff. One previous owner.

370 acres. Call Simon on 09732 1893414.

For those of you who have been affected, we are pleased to say we have finally eradicated Dutch Elm Disease from the community! Well done everybody!

~~SWEDISH~~ ENGLISH MASSAGE

Lowers stress of leaving political unions
Relaxes tension between nations
Targets pains in the neck
Only £15 per 30min session

~~PROFESSIONAL~~ SERVICES
~~Call Freja~~ on 09783 625415
STEVE

MISSING BARISTA

Has anyone seen my lovely barista Goran? He was deported from my local café in early Apr 2019 and now no-one in there knows how to make a decent Latte. Reward offered for safe return. Call Glynis on 09795 268124

09795 268124
09795 268124
09795 268124
09795 268124
09795 268124
09795 268124
09795 268124
09795 268124

POST-BREXIT COMMUNITY HISTORICAL RE-ENACTMENT GROUP

We are currently looking for new recruits to join our next event that will re-enact the signing of the Maastricht Treaty 7th Feb 1992.

Particularly interested in finding someone to play a charismatic John Major!

Email: Joyce@historybuff.brit.uk

ONE WAY

BOARDING PASS

Passenger Name
UNITED KINGDOM

From
THE EU

To
NOWHERE

Carrier
BREXIT AIR

Date
29 MAR 2019

Time
00:00

Flight
EU-027

Seat
55L

Gate
22

Board till
23:59

BOARDING PASS

Passenger Name
UNITED KINGDOM

From
THE EU

To
NOWHERE

Date
29.03.19

Time
00:00

Flight
EU-027

Seat
55L

Gate
22

Board till
23:59

Hi UK !!
We are here at
Oktoberfest having
a wunderbar time!
Sorry you couldn't
make it!

Angela
XXX

HAGEN
TOR
ZUM
SAUERLAND
POSTKARTE

DEUTSCHE BUNDESPOST
10
58

Theresa May
10 Downing St.
London
○ Das England.

Is he a Europhile?

Spot it.
Shop it.
Stop it.

Suspicious?

Call the National Europhilia Watch hotline on 020 0104 2019

BREXIT SMOOTH FINE QUALITY CIGARETTES

MICHAEL GOVE

No. 3 in a series of 12
MAVERICKS OF BREXIT

MICHAEL GOVE
"GOOGLY GOVE"

☒ LEAVER
○ REMAINER

GOOGLY GOVE (OR MERCURIAL MIKE) LEAVES HIS OPPONENTS GUESSING EVERY TIME. WILL HE COME FROM THE LEFT OR WILL HE SNEAK IN ON THE RIGHT? ONE THING'S FOR SURE, HE'LL ALWAYS POP UP AT THE CREASE WHEN HE'S LEAST EXPECTED.

JUST LIKE A COOL BREXIT SMOOTH.

COLLECTABLE CIGARETTE CARDS

← BREXIT

THE BREXIT COLLECTION

A SERIES OF STUNNING STAMPS TO COMMEMORATE THE UK'S EXIT FROM THE EU

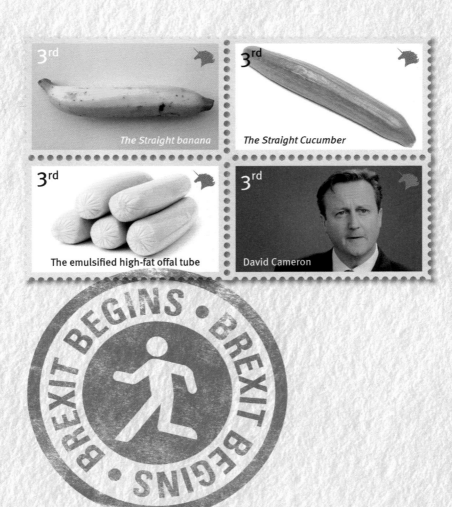

3rd · *The Straight banana*

3rd · *The Straight Cucumber*

3rd · **The emulsified high-fat offal tube**

3rd · David Cameron

BREXIT BEGINS · BREXIT BEGINS · BREXIT BEGINS

nukella

FARRAGO

nukella is the UK's **ONLY** post-Brexit chocolate conker spread.

Launching **Post-Brexit**

The United Kingdom's very own
chocolate jam...

nukella is a delicious blend of British Bournville-style plain chocolate combined with the bitter, smoky crunchiness of British conkers and just a hint of beefy Bovril goodness.

Department of Ongoing Euroscepticism

REDACTED INTELLIGENCE REPORT   CLASSIFIED

MISSION: TO INVESTIGATE POTENTIAL THREAT TO UK CULTURE
AND WAY OF LIFE POST-BREXIT.

SUBJECT: SPAIN

FIELD AGENTS: PENNYWEATHER, J
                        WHITE, D

REPORT AS FOLLOWS:

████████████████████████ Spanish people ████
████ have ██████████ n't ████
████████████████████████ the longest life
expectancy in Europe. ██████████████
████████████████████████████ ██████████
████ ex-pat population is ████████
total ████████████████████████
████████████████████████████
████ bull████████.

HOLIDAYS

all inclusive
Like a bed and breakfast and lunch and dinner and drinks all rolled into one

après ski
Like going to the pub after a very cold day

Alpine chalet
A Swiss mountain caravan with its wheels taken off so it doesn't roll away

EU passport
Like a theme park fast pass or VIP ticket, but for travelling between European countries

Euro Disney
Like Chessington World of Adventures, but where all the animals are played by human beings dressed up

Eurotunnel
Similar to the Dartford Tunnel, but you end up in France, not Dartford

all inclusive

après ski

Alpine chalet

EU passport

Euro Disney

Eurotunnel

HOLIDAYS

flip-flops

A type of footwear worn in European countries where it's warm enough not to wear socks

sand

A substance found on continental beaches instead of pebbles

siesta

An afternoon nap; forty winks

sombrero

A wide-brimmed straw bowler hat, worn to demonstrate you are in (or have been to) Spain

sun cream

Worn in European countries where the sun shines; like salad cream, but for the skin

sunburn

Something that happens in hot European countries, if you don't wear your salad cream (*see above*)

flip-flops

sand

siesta

sombrero

sun cream

sunburn

COINS OF THE EU

Austria

Belgium

Cyprus

Estonia

Finland

France

Germany

Greece

Ireland

Italy

Latvia

Lithuania

Luxembourg

Malta

the Netherlands

Portugal

Slovakia

Slovenia

Spain

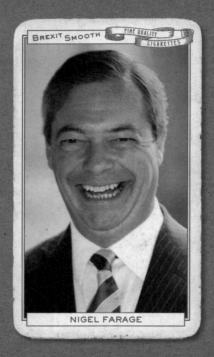

NIGEL FARAGE

No. 4 in a series of 12

MAVERICKS OF BREXIT

NIGEL FARAGE
"THE BUCKING DONKEY"

☒ LEAVER
◯ REMAINER

FARAGE IS A SLIPPERY RIGHT-WINGER WITH A COLOURFUL GIFT OF THE GAB, BOTH ON AND OFF THE PITCH. HE'S ALWAYS HAPPY TO PUT THE BOOT IN BUT SOMEHOW SEEMS TO ESCAPE A SCRAP UNSCATHED. HE'S ALSO A SOCIABLE CHAP, ENJOYING A PINT WITH THE LADS AND RARELY WITHOUT A PACKET OF COOL BREXIT SMOOTH IN HIS CARDIGAN POCKET.

COLLECTABLE CIGARETTE CARDS

Tackling the five stages of Brexit Grief

2. ANGER

Symptoms:

- ✔ High blood pressure
- ✔ Insomnia
- ✔ Irritability towards Leavers
- ✔ Nausea
- ✔ Propensity to throw items at TV sets
- ✔ Inability to contain your darker emotions

Overview

Anger is an overwhelming emotion that can cloud your understanding of rational situations – like Brexit. Whereas before you may have relaxed by watching the news or reading the newspaper, for example, you now find those activities infuriate you and leave you agitated. The anger is born from pain and fear that you have been deserted and abandoned. Face up to that pain, as from anger comes strength.

Treatment

Avoid all media and social networking sites. Live in the moment and focus on the positive if you can find any.

Cure

Time.

 **RHS** Remainers Health Service

BUSES I HAVE SEEN

SH196

Brexit will improve your sex life by 37%

Single deck Volvo B9R
Spotted: July 2017, Bristol

LONDON UNITED RATP GROUP

10 King's Cross

The UK can have its cake and eat it

Double deck Routemaster
diesel-electric hybrid
Spotted: September 2016, London

Single deck Setra S315GT-HD
Spotted: May 2018, Liverpool

Double deck AEC Routemaster RML2760
Spotted: May 2019, Brussels

TREATY ON EUROPEAN UNION

Maastricht, Netherlands
7th February 1992

HIS MAJESTY THE KING OF THE BELGIANS, HER MAJESTY THE QUEEN OF DENMARK, THE PRESIDENT OF THE FEDERAL REPUBLIC OF GERMANY, THE PRESIDENT OF IRELAND, THE PRESIDENT OF THE HELLENIC REPUBLIC, HIS MAJESTY THE KING OF SPAIN, THE PRESIDENT OF THE FRENCH REPUBLIC, THE PRESIDENT OF THE ITALIAN REPUBLIC, HIS ROYAL HIGHNESS THE GRAND DUKE OF LUXEMBOURG, HER MAJESTY THE QUEEN OF THE NETHERLANDS, THE PRESIDENT OF THE PORTUGUESE REPUBLIC, HER MAJESTY THE QUEEN OF THE UNITED KINGDOM OF GREAT BRITAIN AND NORTHERN IRELAND [1],

RESOLVED to mark a new stage in the process of European integration undertaken with the establishment of the European Communities,

DRAWING INSPIRATION from the cultural, religious and humanist inheritance of Europe, from which have developed the universal values of the inviolable and inalienable rights of the human person, freedom, democracy, equality and the rule of law,

RECALLING the historic importance of the ending of the division of the European continent and the need to create firm bases for the construction of the future Europe,

CONFIRMING their attachment to the principles of liberty, democracy and respect for human rights and fundamental freedoms and of the rule of law,

CONFIRMING their attachment to fundamental social rights as defined in the European Social Charter signed at Turin on 18 October 1961 and in the 1989 Community Charter of the Fundamental Social Rights of Workers,

DESIRING to deepen the solidarity between their peoples while respecting their history, their culture and their traditions,

DESIRING to enhance further the democratic and efficient functioning of the institutions so as to enable them better to carry out, within a single institutional framework, the tasks entrusted to them,

RESOLVED to achieve the strengthening and the convergence of their economies and to establish an economic and monetary union including, in accordance with the provisions of this Treaty and of the Treaty on the Functioning of the European Union, a single and stable currency,

DETERMINED to promote economic and social progress for their peoples, taking into account the principle of sustainable development and within the context of the accomplishment of the internal market and of reinforced cohesion and environmental protection, and to implement policies ensuring that advances in economic integration are accompanied by parallel progress in other fields,

RESOLVED to establish a citizenship common to nationals of their countries,

RESOLVED to implement a common foreign and security policy including the progressive framing of a common defence policy, which might lead to a common defence in accordance with the provisions of Article 42, thereby reinforcing the European identity and its independence in order to promote peace, security and progress in Europe and in the world,

RESOLVED to facilitate the free movement of persons, while ensuring the safety and security of their peoples, by establishing an area of freedom, security and justice, in accordance with the provisions of this Treaty and of the Treaty on the Functioning of the European Union,

RESOLVED to continue the process of creating an ever closer union among the peoples of Europe, in which decisions are taken as closely as possible to the citizen in accordance with the principle of subsidiarity,

IN VIEW of further steps to be taken in order to advance European integration,

HAVE DECIDED to establish a European Union and to this end have designated as their Plenipotentiaries:

TREATY ON EUROPEAN UNION

Maastricht, Netherlands
7th February 1992

Signed by

Signed by

Signed by

ON BEHALF OF HIS MAJESTY
THE KING OF THE BELGIANS

ON BEHALF OF THE PRESIDENT
OF THE HELLENIC REPUBLIC

ON BEHALF OF HIS ROYAL HIGHNESS
THE GRAND DUKE OF LUXEMBOURG

Signed by

Signed by

Signed by

ON BEHALF OF HER MAJESTY
THE QUEEN OF DENMARK

ON BEHALF OF HIS MAJESTY
THE KING OF SPAIN

ON BEHALF OF HER MAJESTY
THE QUEEN OF THE NETHERLANDS

Signed by

Signed by

Signed by

ON BEHALF OF THE PRESIDENT
OF THE FEDERAL REPUBLIC OF
GERMANY

ON BEHALF OF THE PRESIDENT
OF THE FRENCH REPUBLIC

ON BEHALF OF THE PRESIDENT
OF THE PORTUGUESE REPUBLIC

Signed by

Signed by

Signed by

ON BEHALF OF
THE PRESIDENT OF IRELAND

ON BEHALF OF THE PRESIDENT
OF THE ITALIAN REPUBLIC

ON BEHALF OF HER MAJESTY
THE QUEEN OF THE UNITED
KINGDOM OF GREAT BRITAIN
AND NORTHERN IRELAND

Don't smuggle
DEATH

KEEP EUROPHILIA
OUT OF BRITAIN

Suspicious?

Call the National Europhilia Watch hotline on 020 0104 2019

STUFF TO
RETURN TO
EUROPE
BEFORE
BREXIT
HAPPY
THU
EVERYDAY
Portuguese men o' war
HAPPY
FRI
EVERYDAY
Spanish fly
Spanish flu
Dutch ovens

BREXIT SMOOTH FINE QUALITY CIGARETTES

JEREMY CORBYN

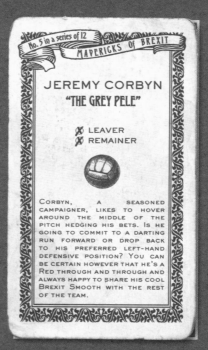

No. 5 in a series of 12

MAVERICKS OF BREXIT

JEREMY CORBYN

"THE GREY PELE"

⊗ LEAVER
⊗ REMAINER

CORBYN, A SEASONED CAMPAIGNER, LIKES TO HOVER AROUND THE MIDDLE OF THE PITCH HEDGING HIS BETS. IS HE GOING TO COMMIT TO A DARTING RUN FORWARD OR DROP BACK TO HIS PREFERRED LEFT-HAND DEFENSIVE POSITION? YOU CAN BE CERTAIN HOWEVER THAT HE'S A RED THROUGH AND THROUGH AND ALWAYS HAPPY TO SHARE HIS COOL BREXIT SMOOTH WITH THE REST OF THE TEAM.

COLLECTABLE CIGARETTE CARDS

← **BREXIT**

THE BREXIT COLLECTION

A SERIES OF STUNNING STAMPS TO COMMEMORATE THE UK'S EXIT FROM THE EU

3rd

The Lying Bus

3rd

On holiday

3rd

The Daily Mail

3rd

Nigel Farage

THE REFERENDUM · THE REFERENDUM

SHOPPING

PRE-BREXIT

POST-BREXIT

Department of Ongoing Euroscepticism

REDACTED INTELLIGENCE REPORT

MISSION: TO INVESTIGATE POTENTIAL THREAT TO UK CULTURE
AND WAY OF LIFE POST-BREXIT.

SUBJECT: DENMARK

FIELD AGENTS: PENNYWEATHER, J
WHITE, D

REPORT AS FOLLOWS:

in Denmark

free university tuition

makes

people

un

happy.

LEGO

is

wrong.

CLASSIFIED

TOP SECRET

BREXIT PRINT

Remember when we were still in the EU and everything was great?
Well now you can re-live those memories EVERY day!

With Brexitprint personalisation you can drink your tea from the Eiffel
Tower and wear Donald Tusk to work. You can move your mouse all over Nigel
Farage's face on your desktop, eat off Jean-Claude Juncker or even go to sleep
under Angela Merkel!

£18·99

£12·99

£5·99

MAKE EU
GREAT AGAIN

£14·99

£8·99

UNITY
SOLIDARITY
HARMONY

£12·99

£9·99

£29·99

*WITH BREXITPRINT
YOU NEED NEVER
LEAVE THE EUROPEAN
UNION AT ALL!*

ARTS & CULTURE

Marcel Marceau
A stripy French Mr. Bean

Brigitte Bardot
Like Samantha Fox but not from London

Salvador Dali
Like Tony Hart but with a curly moustache

ABBA
Sweden's answer to Bucks Fizz, but not alcoholic

'The Killing'
'Midsomer Murders' but with better jumpers

Ingmar Bergman
Like Ken Loach but with subtitles

Puccini's 'Madame Butterfly'
An Italian musical, almost as popular as Queen and Ben Elton's 'We Will Rock You'

Marcel Marceau

Brigitte Bardot

Salvador Dali

ABBA

The Killing

Ingmar Bergman

GLOSSARY OF FORGOTTEN TERMS OF THE EUROPEAN UNION
ARTS & CULTURE

Baudelaire
Like a moany, French Pam Ayres

Hugo Boss
An expensive German BHS but still in business

The Eiffel Tower
Taller version of the Spinnaker tower that provides commanding views of Paris, not Portsmouth

Mona Lisa
Italian picture of a smiling lady, not a British movie starring Bob Hoskins

'Elle' Magazine
A publication of French origin, similar to 'The Lady' but with less emphasis on the Middletons

Puccini's 'Madame Butterfly'

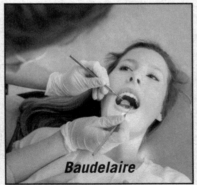
Baudelaire

Hugo Boss

The Eiffel Tower

Mona Lisa

'Elle' Magazine

BREXIT SMOOTH · FINE QUALITY CIGARETTES

ANGELA MERKEL

No. 6 in a series of 12
MAVERICKS OF BREXIT

ANGELA MERKEL
"THE CHANCELLOR"

○ LEAVER
⊗ REMAINER

THIS GERMAN STALWART HAS BEEN AT THE CENTRE OF ANY DEFENCE WORTH TALKING ABOUT FOR DECADES. HER DOMINANCE AS A CENTRE BACK IS FELT ALL ACROSS EUROPE AND SHE'S NOTED FOR HER SOLID AND DEPENDABLE NO-NONSENSE TACKLES AS WELL AS FOR HER FAIR APPROACH TO THE GAME. SHE ALSO HAS A NO-NONSENSE APPROACH TO SMOKING A COOL BREXIT SMOOTH.

COLLECTABLE CIGARETTE CARDS

Tackling the five stages of Brexit Grief

3. BARGAINING

Symptoms:

- ✔ Delusions
- ✔ Abdominal pain
- ✔ Unexpected bouts of haggling
- ✔ Nausea
- ✔ Obsession with foreign exchange rates

Overview

In this stage we are delusional and unrealistic about how to cope with our grief. We will do anything not to feel the pain of Brexit. We remain in the past, trying to negotiate our way out of the hurt. 'If only more young people had voted.' 'Why were the Leavers so blinded by Farage, Gove, the *Daily Mail* and the like?' We are solely preoccupied with 'what if' thoughts.

Treatment

Carry a card with the words 'Yes. Brexit really happened' and refer to it when you feel yourself slipping into a bargaining state.

Cure

None.

 **RHS** Remainers Health Service

2019 MARCH

FEBRUARY 2019

Sun	Mon	Tue	Wed	Thu	Fri	Sat
					1	2
3	4	5	6	7	8	9
10	11	12	13	14	15	16
17	18	19	20	21	22	23
24	25	26	27	28		

APRIL 2019

Sun	Mon	Tue	Wed	Thu	Fri	Sat
	1	2	3	4	5	6
7	8	9	10	11	12	13
14	15	16	17	18	19	20
21	22	23	24	25	26	27
28	29	30				

Sun	Mon	Tue	Wed	Thu	Fri	Sat
					Salon du Chocolat (chocolate festival), Brussels **1**	The Future of Democracy in Europe conference, begins Athens **2**
Bulgaria Liberation Day **3**	**4**	Automotive Tech AD conference, Berlin **5**	The Future of Democracy in Europe conference, ends Athens **6**	Jobmesse Dusseldorf (international education & training industry trade fair) **7**	Festa della Donna, Italy **8**	**9**
10	Lithuanian Independence Day **11**	**12**	**13**	European Parliament plenary session, Brussels **14**	Hungarian Revolution Memorial Day **15**	Malmo Beer and Whisky Festival **16**
St Patrick's Day **17**	Bonfire festival of San José, Valencia **18**	Maltese Feast of St Joseph **19**	**20**	Festa della Primavera, Italy **21**	European Council meeting **22**	Meeting of the German Neuroscience Society, Gottingen **23**
24 Targi Budowlane Lubdom, Poland / British Summer Time begins **31**	Greek Independence Day **25**	Assistive Technology Exhibition, Gothenburg **26**	**27**	Expo Carne, Portugal **28**	Leave the EU!! **29**	**30**

2019
APRIL

MARCH 2019

Sun	Mon	Tue	Wed	Thu	Fri	Sat
					1	2
3	4	5	6	7	8	9
10	11	12	13	14	15	16
17	18	19	20	21	22	23
24/31	25	26	27	28	29	30

MAY 2019

Sun	Mon	Tue	Wed	Thu	Fri	Sat
			1	2	3	4
5	6	7	8	9	10	11
12	13	14	15	16	17	18
19	20	21	22	23	24	25
26	27	28	29	30	31	

Sun	Mon	Tue	Wed	Thu	Fri	Sat
	1	2	3	4	5	6
7	8	9	10	11	12	13
14	15	16	17	18	19	20
21	22	23	24	25 Whale blubber trade show, Greenland	26	27
28	29	30				

WATCH OUT! There's a Europhile about!

Suspicious?

Call the National Europhilia Watch hotline on 020 0104 2019

SORRY YOU'RE LEAVING!

WE'LL MISS YOU!

LETS DO BEERZ SOMETIME

Austria

KEEP ON ROCKIN' DUDE!

NETHERLANDS

KEEP SMILING PAL!

LATVIA

ROMANIA

BoN CHANCE!

FRANCE xxx

YOU WERE AN EFFICIENT AND PRODUCTIVE COLLEAGUE — LUXEMBOURG

See you on the other side!

x Ireland

BEST, GERMANY

ENJOYED WORKING WITH YOU --- BULGARIA

Good Luck in your future endeavours! Sweden X

MALTA ☹

finally got you, you gimp!

DenMark

Miss you fella

Poland x

Lithuania ♡

See you in the summer -
can't wait !
Spain
x

All the best for
the future
love Greece X best Cypress Slovakia
xxxx xxxx

SAD TO SEE
YOU GO

Finland ♥ X X X

Don't be a Stranger! Slovenia
best ITALY X

CROATIA!!

So long!
Hungary

You're crazy LOL !!!
BELGIUM

BEST WISHES
Portugal X

Good luck — you'll need it!
Estonia.

Czech Republic

BREXIT SMOOTH *FINE QUALITY CIGARETTES*

BREXIT SMOOTH *FINE QUALITY CIGARETTES*

JACOB REES-MOGG

No. 7 in a series of 12

MAVERICKS OF BREXIT

JACOB
REES-MOGG

"THE FILIBUSTER"

☒ LEAVER
○ REMAINER

REES-MOGG IS AN OLD-SCHOOL
BATSMAN WHO HAS MADE A
CAREER OF TAKING A TEDIOUS,
ALMOST AGGRESSIVELY DEFENSIVE
STANCE AT THE WICKET. HE'S
ALWAYS HAPPY TO EKE OUT THE
RUNS UNTIL THE OPPORTUNITY
STRIKES TO DRIVE HARD INTO THE
DEEP, DEEP RIGHT MID-WICKET.
REES-MOGG DOESN'T SMOKE
A COOL BREXIT SMOOTH AS HE
HAS NEVER LEARNT HOW TO
INHALE PROPERLY.

COLLECTABLE CIGARETTE CARDS

Make Your Own Pro-European Union

I ♥ EU

I ♥ EU

I ♥ EU

Mini Bunting Kit

Campaign
To Rejoin
The EU

EURP

eurp.eu

Campaign
To Rejoin
The EU

EURP

eurp.eu

Campaign
To Rejoin
The EU

EURP

eurp.eu

Make Your Own Pro-European Union

Mini Bunting Kit

Campaign To Rejoin The EU

eurp.eu

Campaign To Rejoin The EU

eurp.eu

Campaign To Rejoin The EU

eurp.eu

← BREXIT

THE BREXIT COLLECTION

A SERIES OF STUNNING STAMPS TO COMMEMORATE THE UK'S EXIT FROM THE EU

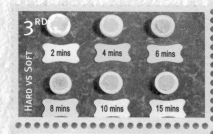

3RD

HARD VS SOFT

2 mins	4 mins	6 mins
8 mins	10 mins	15 mins

3RD

DAVID DAVIS

3RD

ARTICLE 50

3RD

£40-80 BILLION?

THE NEGOTIATION · THE NEGOTIATION · THE NEGOTIATION · THE NEGOTIATION

Department of Ongoing Euroscepticism

REDACTED INTELLIGENCE REPORT   **CLASSIFIED**

MISSION: TO INVESTIGATE POTENTIAL THREAT TO UK CULTURE
AND WAY OF LIFE POST-BREXIT.

SUBJECT: ITALY

FIELD AGENTS: PENNYWEATHER, J
              WHITE, D

REPORT AS FOLLOWS:

Italian ███████████████████████████

████████████ people █████████████████

███████████████████ are ███████████

███████████████ generally hot and dry ████

██████████████████████ because

███████████████████████ of

████████████████████████████

football teams, such as Juventus, Milan and Lazio.

TOP SECRET

UKEA

ENJOY YOUR OUTDOOR SPACE...

At UKEA, we believe in family barbecues, whatever the weather. So, we provide a full range of traditional British outdoor family furniture, ready for a traditional British summer. All our furniture is fully rainproof and suitable for all those long, overcast summer days. Outdoors, the UKEA way...

The Haversham
Functional outside lounger for relaxing in weather.
✔ **British steel** ✔ **Waterproof** ✔ **Rustproof**

£342.00 (p&p £70)

Size: 6ft x 3ft x 1ft / Weight: 4st 10lb
Please allow 15 weeks delivery as this item comes pre-built

The Viscount
Functional outside weather protector for full range weather protection

✔ **British steel and rubberised cotton**
✔ **Waterproof/windproof/snowproof**
✔ **Rustproof** ✔ **Concrete base** ✔ **Non-portable**

£563.00 (p&p £70)

Size: 7ft x 6ft circumference / Weight: 2st 7lb
Please allow 15 weeks delivery as this item comes pre-built

The Country Seat
Functional all-weather gazebo with full range weather protection

✔ **Pig Iron and British kite-marked glass**
✔ **Waterproof/windproof/snowproof**
✔ **Rustproof** ✔ **Concrete floor** ✔ **Capable of withstanding Beaufort storm force 10 conditions**

£18032.00 (p&p £1000)

Size: 15ft x 10ft x 8ft / Weight: 4 tons
Please allow 4 years delivery as this item comes pre-built

The Churchill
Functional metal table and chairs for outside dining

✔ **British Steel and rubberised cotton**
✔ **Waterproof/windproof/snowproof**
✔ **Rustproof** ✔ **Fun**

£5624.00 (p&p £700)

Size: Table 15ft x 4ft x 4ft / Chairs 5ft x 2ft x 2ft / Weight: Table 1 ton
Please allow 18 months delivery as this item comes pre-built

The Whimsy
Functional foldable chair for use at coastlines

✔ **Mahogany and rubberised cotton**
✔ **Waterproof/windproof/snowproof**
✔ **Only 45 minutes assembly time**

£567.00 (p&p £89)

Size: 7ft x 4ft x 3ft / Weight: 4st
Please allow 6 months delivery as this item comes pre-built

PRESENTS ...

20 ESSENTIAL BREAK-UP 'BREX-HITS' FROM THE 80s AND 90s

WALLOW IN THE EXQUISITE PAIN OF BREAKING UP
WITH THE EU AND SOOTHE AWAY THOSE BREXIT BLUES WITH
THIS ULTIMATE COLLECTION OF TWENTY TEAR-JERKING TRACKS

I Will Always Love You
WHITNEY HOUSTON

Too Late for Goodbyes
JULIAN LENNON

Leaving Me Now
LEVEL 42

So Lonely
THE POLICE

Un-Break My Heart
TONI BRAXTON

Nothing Compares 2 U
SINEAD O'CONNOR

It Must Have Been Love
ROXETTE

Goodbye
THE SPICE GIRLS

When You're Gone
THE CRANBERRIES

**Don't Leave
Me This Way**
THE COMMUNARDS

Don't Go
HOTHOUSE FLOWERS

Don't You (Forget About Me)
SIMPLE MINDS

Stay
SHAKESPEARS SISTER

I Think We're Alone Now
TIFFANY

**Heaven Knows
I'm Miserable Now**
THE SMITHS

Only When You Leave
SPANDAU BALLET

One More Night
PHIL COLLINS

The King Of Wishful Thinking
GO WEST

Borderline
MADONNA

Come Back And Stay
PAUL YOUNG

BREXIT SMOOTH

FINE QUALITY CIGARETTES

BREXIT SMOOTH — FINE QUALITY CIGARETTES

DAVID DAVIS

No. 8 in a series of 12 — MAVERICKS OF BREXIT

DAVID DAVIS
"THE GHOST"

☒ LEAVER
○ REMAINER

A LIGHTWEIGHT WHO IS KNOWN FOR USING AVOIDANCE TACTICS IN THE RING. DAVIS IS AN EVASIVE CHARACTER, WHO CREATES THE IMPRESSION OF WORKING HARD WHILST ACTUALLY DOING VERY LITTLE, THEREBY WEARING HIS OPPONENT DOWN. HE IS KNOWN AS 'THE GHOST', JUST LIKE THE SMOKE FROM A COOL BREXIT SMOOTH.

COLLECTABLE CIGARETTE CARDS

Tackling the five stages of Brexit Grief

4. DEPRESSION

Symptoms:

✔ Lethargy
✔ Migraine
✔ Lack of appetite
✔ Feelings of desperation

Overview

We often get depressed after a loss and sometimes it's considered unnatural: something to just deal with. But it's important to remember that the loss of a cross-continent union is a depressing situation and depression is an appropriate response. The relationships you had with all those countries has been ripped away from you and you are justified in feeling emotionally distraught.

Treatment

Anti-depressants in addition to cognitive behavioural therapy (CBT). A therapist can help you identify negative or false thoughts and replace those thoughts with healthier, more realistic ones. Such as 'We are living in a post-Brexit UK, now accept this'.

Cure

None.

 **RHS** Remainers Health Service

GARDEN VIEW

PRE-BREXIT

POST-BREXIT

GLOSSARY OF FORGOTTEN TERMS OF THE EUROPEAN UNION
DRINK

café au lait
An all-milk Mellow Birds instant coffee

champagne
A type of French Pomagne, but made with grapes, not apples

cognac
An alcoholic after-dinner drink for posh old men; tastes a bit like Benylin

tripel trappistenbier
Like a pint of strong bitter, but made in Belgium by vicars

espresso
Three heaped spoonfuls of Mellow Birds without any milk, served in a tiny weeny children's cup

kir royale
A French version of snakebite & black that isn't just drunk by goths

café au lait

champagne

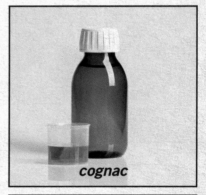

cognac

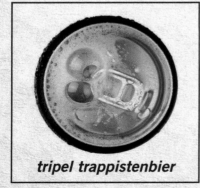

tripel trappistenbier

espresso

kir royale

DRINK

Orangina
Fizzy orange squash but with bits at the bottom of the bottle

limoncello
An Italian after-dinner drink; looks like lemon toilet cleaner, but not as poisonous

ouzo
Aniseed balls but in Greek liquid form

Perrier
A type of tap water that comes out of the ground fizzy, like a natural Sodastream; sold in green bottles to make it more expensive

schnapps
Very strong, see-through alcohol, served in small glasses so you can drink it quicker

wine
Like Schloer, but with alcohol added to it

Orangina

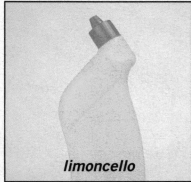
limoncello

ouzo

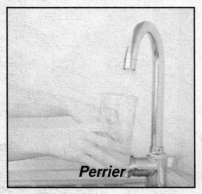
Perrier

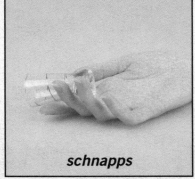
schnapps

wine

TREATY ON THE FUNCTIONING OF THE EUROPEAN UNION

Rome, Italy
25th March 1957

HIS MAJESTY THE KING OF THE BELGIANS, THE PRESIDENT OF THE FEDERAL REPUBLIC OF GERMANY, THE PRESIDENT OF THE FRENCH REPUBLIC, THE PRESIDENT OF THE ITALIAN REPUBLIC, HER ROYAL HIGHNESS THE GRAND DUCHESS OF LUXEMBOURG, HER MAJESTY THE QUEEN OF THE NETHERLANDS,

DETERMINED to lay the foundations of an ever-closer union among the peoples of Europe,

RESOLVED to ensure the economic and social progress of their countries by common action to eliminate the barriers which divide Europe,

AFFIRMING as the essential objective of their efforts the constant improvement of the living and working conditions of their peoples,

RECOGNISING that the removal of existing obstacles calls for concerted action in order to guarantee steady expansion, balanced trade and fair competition,

ANXIOUS to strengthen the unity of their economies and to ensure their harmonious development by reducing the differences existing between the various regions and the backwardness of the less favoured regions,

DESIRING to contribute, by means of a common commercial policy, to the progressive abolition of restrictions on international trade,

INTENDING to confirm the solidarity which binds Europe and the overseas countries and desiring to ensure the development of their prosperity, in accordance with the principles of the Charter of the United Nations,

RESOLVED by thus pooling their resources to preserve and strengthen peace and liberty, and calling upon the other peoples of Europe who share their ideal to join in their efforts,

HAVE DECIDED to create a European Economic Community and to this end have designated as their Plenipotentiaries:

TREATY ON THE FUNCTIONING OF THE EUROPEAN UNION

Rome, Italy
25th March 1957

Signed

....

ON BEHALF OF HIS MAJESTY
THE KING OF THE BELGIANS

Signed

....

ON BEHALF OF THE PRESIDENT
OF THE ITALIAN REPUBLIC

Signed

....

ON BEHALF OF THE PRESIDENT
OF THE FEDERAL REPUBLIC OF GERMANY

Signed

....

ON BEHALF OF HER ROYAL HIGHNESS
THE GRAND DUCHESS OF LUXEMBOURG

Signed

....

ON BEHALF OF THE PRESIDENT
OF THE FRENCH REPUBLIC

Signed

....

ON BEHALF OF HER MAJESTY
THE QUEEN OF THE NETHERLANDS

Coughs and sneezes spread Europhilia

EUROPHILIA WATCH

always carry tissues

cover your face

throw used tissues away

clean your hands every 4 seconds

Stop Europhilia spreading

Call the National Europhilia Watch hotline on 020 0104 2019

NICK CLEGG

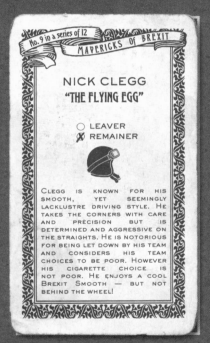

No. 9 in a series of 12 · MAVERICKS OF BREXIT

NICK CLEGG
"THE FLYING EGG"

○ LEAVER
⊗ REMAINER

CLEGG IS KNOWN FOR HIS SMOOTH, YET SEEMINGLY LACKLUSTRE DRIVING STYLE. HE TAKES THE CORNERS WITH CARE AND PRECISION BUT IS DETERMINED AND AGGRESSIVE ON THE STRAIGHTS. HE IS NOTORIOUS FOR BEING LET DOWN BY HIS TEAM AND CONSIDERS HIS TEAM CHOICES TO BE POOR. HOWEVER HIS CIGARETTE CHOICE IS NOT POOR. HE ENJOYS A COOL BREXIT SMOOTH — BUT NOT BEHIND THE WHEEL!

COLLECTABLE CIGARETTE CARDS

CARTE POSTALE

Certains pays étrangers n'acceptant pas la correspondance de ce côté, se renseigner à la Poste

Correspondance

Adresse

Dear Theresa,
wish "EU"
were here!

Emmanuel

Mr THERESA MAY
10 DOWNING ST.
ANGLETERRE
G. BRETAGNE

PARIS-R.P.
10
AOUT
DISTRIBON

MORE
COINS OF THE EU

Bulgaria

Croatia

Czech Republic

Denmark

Hungary

Poland

Romania

Sweden

United Kingdom

Department of Ongoing Euroscepticism

CLASSIFIED

CLASSIFIED

REDACTED INTELLIGENCE REPORT

MISSION: TO INVESTIGATE POTENTIAL THREAT TO UK CULTURE
AND WAY OF LIFE POST-BREXIT.

SUBJECT: GREECE

FIELD AGENTS: PENNYWEATHER, J
               WHITEXXXX
               [M.I.A. — LAST KNOWN LOCATION ROME, ITALY]

REPORT AS FOLLOWS:

Greek ████████████████████████
████ famously low cost of living ████████
████ a ████████████ is ████████
██████████████████████████████
myths and legends. ████████ lot of old
████████████████████████ no
████████ one ████████████████
████████████ likes ████████
████████████████████████
feta cheese.

TOP SECRET

Gentlemen, engage your gear sticks...
Welcome to a new **era** of British cars.

The Farragi Borderlander

Built in Britain. By Britain. For Britain.

Engineering

For fastness…
For start-ability…
with sensitive pothole recovery suspension…
with UK-only GPS as standard…

Prestige

In the Borderlander you are untouchable,
independent, a person of interest…

Luxury

The distinctive cockpit offers
every conceivable comfort,
with a driver's pint glass-holder…
and with ashtrays in every seat.

Drive independently. Drive…

farragi

GAMES NIGHT

PRE-BREXIT

POST-BREXIT

BREXIT SMOOTH FINE QUALITY CIGARETTES

PAUL DACRE

No. 10 in a series of 12
MAVERICKS OF BREXIT

PAUL DACRE
"THE BELGRAVIA RAVER"

⊗ LEAVER
○ REMAINER

DACRE IS A HUGELY POPULAR
MIDDLEWEIGHT WITH AN UGLY BUT
HIGHLY EFFECTIVE STYLE. HE
SLUGS AWAY AT HIS OPPONENT IN
A BARRAGE OF JABS AND
UPPERCUTS AND IS FREQUENTLY
PENALIZED FOR PUNCHING BELOW
THE BELT. AND THE BELT
IS USUALLY WHERE HE LIKES TO
KEEP HIS COOL BREXIT SMOOTH
CIGARETTES.

COLLECTABLE CIGARETTE CARDS

EURO PHILIA

Don't die of Europhilia

Political and economic intimacy costs lives

Suspicious?

Call the National Europhilia Watch hotline on 020 0104 2019

Post-Brexit
Community Notices

PLEASE NOTE:
ABBA TRIBUTE ACT 'ABBATASTIC' SCHEDULED FOR SAT 12TH OCT IS NOW CANCELLED.

DELIGHTED TO ANNOUNCE THE CONFIRMED BOOKING OF 'THE AUSTRALIAN WURZELS' AS REPLACEMENT

CLEANER WANTED

I'm looking for someone to clean up a large mess left by David Cameron. Must be professional, courteous
.

£10+ per hour

Call Barry 09791 625196

NEED AN EXPERIENCED NEGOTIATOR?

Then look no further.
All jobs considered, big or small - from 'argument in Wickes car park' to 'fallout with continental union'.
References on request. Low price guaranteed.
DBS checked and good with pets. Available April 2019.

Call Dave (Davis) on 09739 812789

WANTED

REPLACEMENT ROTATING ARM FOR BOSCH CLASSIX DISHWASHER. CAN'T FIND ONE ANYWHERE AND DISHES ARE STACKING UP.

CALL LINDA ON 09142 6712334

FOR SALE

4 Bedroom House

We are having to return to Italy unexpectedly and so, unfortunately have to sell our beautiful family home. Sold as seen, furniture, fixtures and fittings included.

~~£480,000~~

ONLY £300,000   ~~£430,000~~

Call Antonio on 01288 672345 to arrange a viewing.

English Language Classes Offered

Come and learn English in the land of Shakespear and Jeffrey Archer. Extra special rates for groups after a massive cancellation. Morris dancing classes also available.
Call Lawrence 09862 146588

Please note that the Village Fête has now been renamed the Village Fate

Nurses Needed!!
starting April 2019
Up to 20,000 nurses needed urgently to fill hastily vacated roles in the NHS.
No experience necessary.
Call Larry on 01288 664509

unity
solidarity
harmony

adieu

I ♥ EU

Single deck Setra S 415
Spotted: April 2018, Dungeness

Double deck Alexander
Dennis Enviro 400
Spotted: February 2016, London

Single deck Scania Irizar (?)
Spotted: May 2016, Lake District

Single deck Setra S 415
Spotted: April 2018, Dungeness

EUROPEAN WORDS WE CAN NO LONGER USE

bon voyage (French)
A pretentious way of saying 'have a nice trip'. *Use instead:* 'have a nice trip'

déjà vu (French)
The uncanny feeling that you're doing or seeing something you've already done or seen before. *Use instead:* 'already seen this'

déjà vu (French)
The uncanny feeling that you're doing or seeing something you've already done or seen before. *Use instead:* 'already seen this'

double entendre (French)
When someone (usually in a 'Carry On' film) says something that sounds a bit smutty. *Use instead:* 'oooh, matron!'

doppelgänger (German)
People who look so much alike, often a harbinger of bad luck. *Use instead:* 'Jedward'

faux pas (French)
An embarrassing blunder, such as a referendum on Britain leaving the EU. *Use instead:* 'doing a Cameron'

bon voyage

déjà vu

déjà vu

double entendre

doppelgänger

faux pas

EUROPEAN WORDS WE CAN NO LONGER USE

kindergarten *(German)*
Another word for a pre-school nursery, literally means 'garden of Kinder Surprise'. *Use instead:* 'Creme Eggarten'

lingerie *(French)*
A type of impractical undergarment, usually purchased as a present for a woman by a hopeful man. *Use instead:* 'kecks'

ménage à trois *(French)*
A type of intimate friendship between three people. *Use instead:* Ken & Deirdre Barlow/Mike Baldwin

smörgåsbord *(Swedish)*
A table with too many different types of food on it. *Use instead:* 'all you can eat carvery'

status quo *(Latin)*
Something that never changes – it stays the same forever and ever, even when a member of the band dies. *Use instead:* 'Fleetwood Mac'

uber *(German)*
A type of online taxi that can go south of the river at any time of day or night. *Use instead:* 'the nightbus'

kindergarten

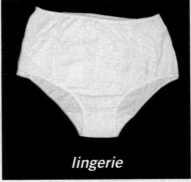

lingerie

ménage à trois

smörgåsbord

status quo

uber

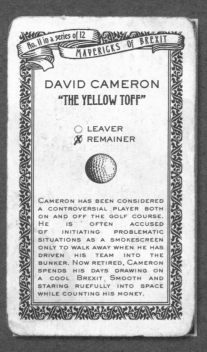

No. 11 in a series of 12 — MAVERICKS OF BREXIT

DAVID CAMERON
"THE YELLOW TOFF"

○ LEAVER
⊗ REMAINER

CAMERON HAS BEEN CONSIDERED A CONTROVERSIAL PLAYER BOTH ON AND OFF THE GOLF COURSE. HE IS OFTEN ACCUSED OF INITIATING PROBLEMATIC SITUATIONS AS A SMOKESCREEN ONLY TO WALK AWAY WHEN HE HAS DRIVEN HIS TEAM INTO THE BUNKER. NOW RETIRED, CAMERON SPENDS HIS DAYS DRAWING ON A COOL BREXIT, SMOOTH AND STARING RUEFULLY INTO SPACE WHILE COUNTING HIS MONEY.

DAVID CAMERON

COLLECTABLE CIGARETTE CARDS

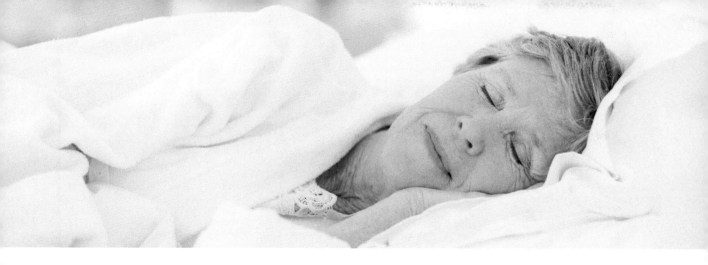

Tackling the five stages of Brexit Grief

5. ACCEPTANCE

Symptoms:

✔ Peacefulness
✔ Ability to eat saucisson sec without weeping
✔ Euphoria
✔ Resolve

Overview

Acceptance, the last of the five stages of grief, can be confusing. People feel that they should feel okay again, like they felt before the loss of their beloved political and economic union. However, most people don't feel okay again. They feel different. The difference being that they are still grieving but that they can now cope better. They don't like the fact that the EU is physically gone but they are able to accept it.

Treatment

Be at peace with your acceptance of Brexit. Recognise your feelings.

Cure

You're cured.

 **RHS** Remainers Health Service

Stuff we've borrowed from France that needs to go back:

French kissing

French letters

French windows

French horns

French fries

French cricket

French poodles

French manicure

French dressing

French plait

The phrase 'pardon my French'

Dawn French

Stuff France has borrowed from us that we need to get back:

Crème anglaise

Cor anglais

If you think of anything else they've borrowed,
pop it on the list. Thanks!

Department of Ongoing Euroscepticism

CLASSIFIED

REDACTED INTELLIGENCE REPORT

MISSION: TO INVESTIGATE POTENTIAL THREAT TO UK CULTURE
AND WAY OF LIFE POST-BREXIT.

CLASSIFIED

SUBJECT: GERMANY

FIELD AGENTS: PENNYWEATHER, J
               NEWMAN, G

REPORT AS FOLLOWS:

████████████████████████████████
Merkel ██████████████████████████   Angela
█████████████████████████████████████
████████████████████████
███████████████████████████████████
███████████████████████████████████
███████████████████████████████████
█ smells ███████████████████████████████
████████████████

TOP SECRET

ENJOY YOUR MEAL...

UKEA

After a successful UKEA shopping spree, why not relax and enjoy a British family meal in our UKEA British family restaurant? All our ingredients are sourced in the UK and represent the best traditional British food available at an appropriate post-Brexit price. Food, the UKEA way...

The Full English
£18 (with tea add £5)

The Full Swedish
£24 (not available with tea)

For Mains...

This month's special!
Celebrating our international friends:

Japan

British Swedish-style meatballs (faggots) with chips, peas and gravy

£32 (with tea add £5)

A sizzling selection of white bread sandwiches containing margarine and meat

£14

Sushi & chips

£41 (with free tap water in glass)

For the veggie ...

Peas in a bowl

£18 (with tea add £5)

Lettuce surprise

£18 (with tea add £5)

For afters ...

British apple crumble
Served with a choice of either evaporated milk, UHT squirty-cream or warm custard

£18

British Spotted Dick

£11

For the kids ...

Hastings winkles

£12 (with sugary tea add £5)

Bangers and mash

£15 (with sugary tea add £5)

Drinks

Lake District water	£5
English tea	£5

HOLIDAYS

PRE-BREXIT

POST-BREXIT

PRESENTS ...

**20 ESSENTIAL
MILLENNIAL BREAK-UP
'BREX-HITS'**

WALLOW IN THE EXQUISITE PAIN OF A BROKEN HEART
AND SOOTHE AWAY THOSE BREXIT BLUES WITH THIS
ULTIMATE COLLECTION OF TWENTY TEAR-JERKING TRACKS

Stay With Me
SAM SMITH

Best Thing I Never Had
BEYONCÉ

Love You, Goodbye
ONE DIRECTION

Goodbye My Lover
JAMES BLUNT

Please Don't Leave Me
PINK

We Are Never, Ever
Getting Back Together
TAYLOR SWIFT

Somebody That
I Used To Know
GOTYE

We Don't Talk Anymore
**CHARLIE PUTH
AND SELENA GOMEZ**

Goodbye, Goodbye
TEGAN AND SARA

Let It Go
JAMES BAY

You Need Me,
I Don't Need You
ED SHEERAN

No Tears Left To Cry
ARIANA GRANDE

Since U Been Gone
KELLY CLARKSON

We Belong Together
MARIAH CAREY

The One That
Got Away
KATY PERRY

No Goodbyes
DUA LIPA

I'll Be Missing You
**PUFF DADDY
& FAITH EVANS**

I Miss You
CLEAN BANDIT

Too Good To Say Goodbye
BRUNO MARS

Sorry
JUSTIN BIEBER

GORDON BROWN

No. 12 in a series of 12

MAVERICKS OF BREXIT

GORDON BROWN
"GRABBER GORDON"

○ LEAVER
⊗ REMAINER

THIS FORMIDABLE SCOTTISH NUMBER ONE BRAVELY PROPPED UP THE FRONT ROW AND COULD HANDLE HIMSELF IN THE RUCK AND MAUL, UNTIL HIS TEAM CRASHED OUT OF THE TOURNAMENT. ALTHOUGH HE HAS BOWED OUT OF THE PROFESSIONAL GAME HE STILL DRIVES THE PACK FORWARD WHEN WHEELED OUT FOR THE ODD TESTIMONIAL OR TWO. HE'S ALSO MORE THAN KEEN TO OFFER A TESTIMONIAL WHEN IT COMES TO THE COOL DRAW OF A BREXIT SMOOTH.

COLLECTABLE CIGARETTE CARDS

←BREXIT

THE
BREXIT
COLLECTION

**A SERIES OF STUNNING STAMPS
TO COMMEMORATE THE UK'S
EXIT FROM THE EU**

3RD POST-BREXIT BUSINESS

3RD POST-BREXIT CUISINE

3RD POST-BREXIT HOLIDAYS

3RD THE LAST LAUGH

THE AFTERMATH · THE AFTERMATH

BRENTRANCE →

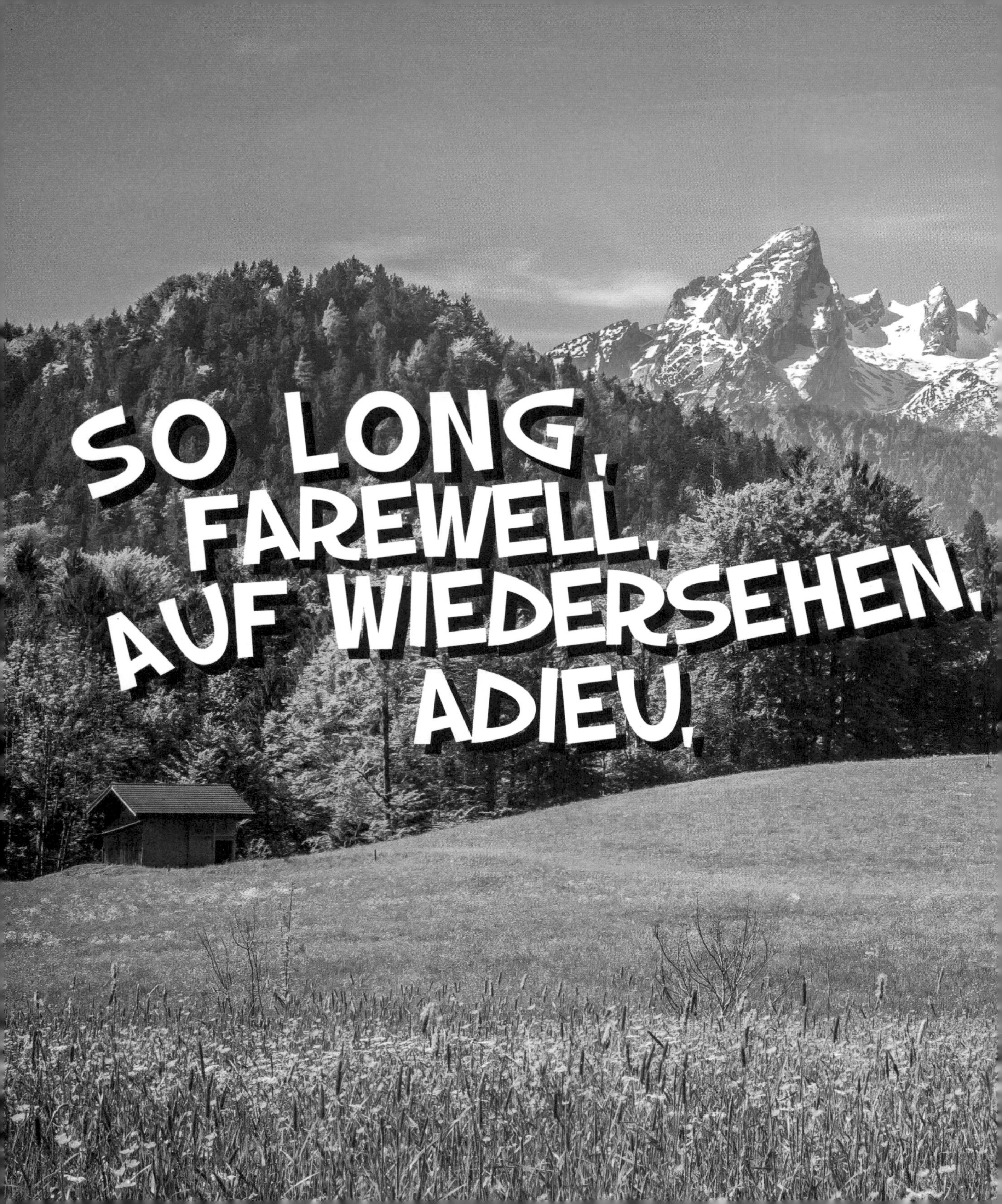
SO LONG,
FAREWELL,
AUF WIEDERSEHEN,
ADIEU.

ADIEU, ADIEU,
TO EU AND EU
AND EU

EUROPEAN UNION

UNITED KINGDOM OF
GREAT BRITAIN
AND NORTHERN IRELAND

PASSPORT

Fold Flap

Fold Flap

Fold Flap

Fold Flap

Fold Flap

Fold Flap

Fashion your own burgundy passport cover from the template above

SOME NATIONAL FLOWERS
of the
EUROPEAN UNION

Find samples of these flowers and press them between the pages of this book as a keepsake of good times in the Union.

AUSTRIA
Edelweiss
(*Leontopodium Alpinum*)

BELGIUM
Red Poppy
(*Papaver Rhoeas*)

BULGARIA
Rose
(*Rosa*)

CROATIA
Iris
(Iris Croatica)

CYPRUS
Cyclamen
(Cyclamen Cyprium)

ESTONIA
Cornflower
(Centaurea Cyanus)

FINLAND
Lily-of-the Valley
(*Convallaria Majalis*)

GREECE
Bear's Breech
(*Acanthus Mollis*)

IRELAND
Shamrock
(*Trifolium Dubium*)

LATVIA
Oxeye Daisy
(*Leucanthemum Vulgare*)

NETHERLANDS
Tulip
(*Tulipa*)

PORTUGAL
Lavender
(*Lavandula Spica*)

ROMANIA
Dog Rose
(Rosa Canina)

SWEDEN
Twinflower
(Linnea Borealis)

SLOVENIA
Red Carnation
(Dianthus Caryophyllus)

Photo Credits:

Alamy.com: *page 62, Matthew Chattle; page 94, Glyn Genin.*

Shutterstock.com: *page 8, Twocoms; page 14, Frederic Legrand – COMEO; page 24, Twocoms; page 25, 360b; page 34, Twocoms; page 38, Frederic Legrand – COMEO; page 44, Twocoms; page 45 (top left), Jakub Junek; page 45 (top right), Dominic Dudley; page 45 (bottom left), Hadrian; page 45 (bottom right), Alexandros Michailidis; page 50 (top left), Marcin Kadziolka; page 50 (top right), Cyril Hou; page 51 (top left), Bangkruayan; page 51 (middle), Stuart Boulton; page 51 (bottom left), Frederic Legrand – COMEO; page 52 (top middle), Corepics VOF; page 52 (bottom left), Featureflash Photo Agency; page 52 (bottom right), Andrea Raffin; page 53 (top left), Andrea Raffin; page 53 (bottom middle), Denis Makarenko; page 53 (bottom right), Featureflash Photo Agency; page 54, Frederic Legrand – COMEO; page 67 (top right), Alexandros Michailidis; page 74, Twocoms; page 78 (bottom right), Julia Suvorova; page 80, 360b; page 84, twocoms; page 102 (top middle), Alexandros Michailidis; page 102 (bottom right), Featureflash Photo Agency; page 103 (top left), 360b; page 103 (bottom middle), JStone; page 104 MediaPictures.pl; page 116, 360b; page 117 (bottom right), Twocoms.*

Credits

Proofreading: *Ian Allen*